DIE! DIE! DIE! OLD PEOPLE DIE!

Jon Haynes & David Woods

DIE! DIE! DIE! OLD PEOPLE DIE!

OBERON BOOKS
LONDON

WWW.OBERONBOOKS.COM

First published in 2019 by Oberon Books Ltd
521 Caledonian Road, London N7 9RH
Tel: +44 (0) 20 7607 3637 / Fax: +44 (0) 20 7607 3629
e-mail: info@oberonbooks.com
www.oberonbooks.com

PB ISBN: 9781786828361
E ISBN: 9781786828378

Cover image: Bryony Jackson

Printed and bound by 4EDGE Limited, Hockley, Essex, UK.
eBook conversion by Lapiz Digital Services, India.

10 9 8 7 6 5 4 3 2 1

Die! Die! Die! Old People Die! received its world premiere at Arts House, Melbourne, 20th November 2018, and its UK premiere at Battersea Arts Centre, 8th May 2019.

NORMAN   David Woods

VIOLET / ARTHUR   Jon Haynes

Written and directed by Jon Haynes and David Woods

Script and Performance Collaborators: Renee Lim, Richard Talbot, Rupert Jones, Janie Booth, Arthur Bolkas, Minsun Park, Patrizia Paolini, GLYPT workshop, Arend Tjepkema and Pheline Thierens, Keenan Groom, Anna Makepeace, Jordan Sim, Roisin McDonnell

Movement Consultant: Thomas Bradley

Elderhood Consultant: Ailsa Richardson

Biomedical Consultants: Anne Cooke and Professor Peter Kinderman

Design: Romanie Harper

Design Assistant: Bethany Fellowes

Lighting: Richard Vabre

Sound: Marco Cher-Gibard

Dogs: Clancy Kriegler, Onion Fellowes, Finn Oakes

Production Manager: Suzy Somerville

Originally Produced by Erin Milne, Bureau of Works, Melbourne

Press and PR: Ben Starick, Martha Oakes and Sue Lancashire

Film: Takeshi Kondo, Phil Moran

Photography: Stuart Patterson and Bryony Jackson

Thank You

The Albany, Boris Belay, Artists Commons Brussels, Siteworks, John Gorick, Arlington Arts Centre, Finn, Greenwich and Lewisham Young People's Theatre, Komedia, The Caribbean Social Forum, Norman Saunders-White, Neiro, Roger Somerville, Professor Peter Kinderman and Anne Cooke; Angharad Wynne-Jones, Josh Wright, Asha Bee Abraham; Emily Sexton, Olivia Anderson and all at Arts House, Melbourne; Richard Dufty, Shelley Hastings and all at Battersea Arts Centre; Kate Yedigaroff and all at Mayfest; Dr. Richard Talbot and students at the University of Salford and to our families for their inspiration, understanding and love.

Acknowledgements

Die! Die! Die! Old People Die! has been supported by the Australian Government through the Australia Council for the Arts, National Lottery through Arts Council England, a Wellcome Trust Arts Award and the City of Melbourne through Arts House and its Culture Lab programme. It has been co-commissioned by Battersea Arts Centre, Arts House and The Albany.

Drawings by David Woods and Stanley Woods.

First we see Norman.

He is one hundred and twenty years old and he is decked out in full evening dress, complete with burgundy coloured cummerbund.

A portion of a white dress shirt peeks out through his half done up flies.

His abdomen is distended and his back is hunched due to degenerative narrowing of the spinal canal.

Then we see Violet.

She is hanging onto his right arm.

Her white hair falls down over her face and she is wearing a pendulous pearl necklace, an off-white jacket with mother of pearl buttons and a lilac-coloured evening dress that completely covers her feet.

A patent leather brown handbag is dangling from her right hand. It has a clasp on it and a price tag attached to the handle by a short piece of string.

There is the sound of a clock ticking.

Once Norman and Violet have composed themselves they turn to look at the audience. They seem to be looking through them, far into the distance. Then they direct their gaze inwards, as if reflecting on their lives.

Their faces are white and pasty, as though regularly dusted with fine white powder. Norman gapes. His mouth is like a deep infected gash in a piece of flesh. His tongue appears flattened. We never see his teeth.

Eventually they turn their attention to the journey they intend to make towards a circular extending dining table that's situated in the foreground of the room.

It's fashioned from mahogany, and hanging over it is a five-tier wedding cake chandelier with a crystal top. On the table is a glass of water. There are two chairs with sturdy legs and well-defined claw and ball feet, one of them at the head of the table, and the other one at the side.

Beneath the table is a rug of sixteenth century Persian design that incorporates a leaf lattice pattern enclosing a variety of oriental shrubs, with muskmelon at the crossover of the lattice and alternating weeping pear and mulberry tree motifs.

Norman proceeds with unsteady movements, placing his feet carefully on the ground before him as if he is feeling his way. Each step is preceded and accompanied by gargantuan effort he is at great pains to conceal.

Violet's deportment is even more strained than her husband's. She displays such extreme concavity of the spine that it looks as though she has been tasked with carrying an invisible chair behind her, about six inches away from her back, and instructed to keep it suspended there at all costs. She appears to be so burdened by the weight of this imaginary article of furniture that she sinks further and further into the floor.

She stops to brush some hair from her face that is irritating her skin.

She stops again to scratch the tip of her desiccated nose.

Norman pauses to accommodate her scratching and once it's complete they shuffle on.

The clock chimes.

They pause, looking out again, counterbalanced off each other's arms and on the point of toppling over, before continuing their way towards the table.

They hesitate a few times as if lost, and look around, wondering if they've taken a wrong turning. They haven't. It's just that they are hypersensitive to noises both inside and outside the room – a tram turning the corner and screeching, a person coughing, a baby crying.

When they approach the table, Norman pulls out her chair and they work together to try and get her seated.

Their combined efforts, rather than bringing her closer to the table, only succeed in moving her further away from it.

Eventually, she manages to extend her handbag so that it hovers a few inches above the table's surface and she is able to execute its tentative descent.

When settled, the man stands at the lady's side and they both look out at the audience, preparing themselves to make some kind of formal address.

His voice is high and rasping and at first it's quite difficult to understand what he is saying. It's possible he has one lung.

He says: I just wanted to say.

She says in a similar, though slightly weaker, register: Lovely. Lovely.

He listens.

She says: Lovely.

He says: How lovely it is to be in this room with all of you beautiful people.

He looks at someone in particular, thinking they look familiar, and that he has just spotted them for the first time.

He says: This is a very special day for all of us. And we are… what?

She says: Hmm?

He says: Super excited, humbled, grateful and of course honoured to share it with such charming, witty and intelligent friends. You have been an endlessly thoughtful, ever so brilliant and – most importantly for us – heroically interesting presence.

She says: Bravo!

He says: It is a total…

He falters, turns and makes a tortuously slow trip to a tall metal cabinet that stands against the wall. It has 'Inlet – outlet valve' imprinted on it.

He opens its doors and then, after rotating and inclining his torso so that his posterior is settled comfortably inside, promptly breaks wind into it.

Satisfied, he turns, closes the door, turns again and makes his way back to the table.

He says: It is a total delight…

She says: Lovely.

He says: Shall I open the window?

She says: That would be lovely.

She raises her right hand and leaves it suspended in mid- air.

He goes towards the window and looks up, a movement that triggers a violent coughing fit.

He reaches for a hanky from his left jacket pocket and pulls out a sock instead.

He hoists his trousers for a moment and sees that it matches the sock on his left foot and that he has no sock on his right.

He casts a glance back in her direction and opens up the sock to spit into it.

He misses, and the expectorant splats onto the floor.

She says: Lovely. All lovely talented people. Lovely.

He collects himself and puts his sock away.

He says: It is a total delight. It is a total delight… Full stop. This building…

She revs up her legs underneath the table, then rises and begins to make her way towards the cabinet.

Once she has passed him she swings her arms energetically at her sides as if striding purposefully while actually rooted to the spot.

Somehow, though, she makes some progress, and when she reaches the cabinet she opens it and turns around, aiming to fart directly into it.

She turns, assuming that she has done so, closes the door, deftly fans away escaping gas and makes her way back to the table at what might be called her normal pace.

Norman watches her, though he seems to have drifted off. His eyes roll back into his head.

Violet sits down.

He says: This building… this building screams of joyous wonder… of vanities and dynasties, of love and war, of criminal ambition and our collective ability to lift beyond the everyday. To gawp.

She says: Lovely

He says: Darling?

She says: Lovely. Lovely. All Beautiful. Wonderful people. Happy. Lovely talented hubby. Kiss.

He says: *(To her.)* Talented wifey.

She says: Not at all.

He says: Kiss kiss.

He presents her with a flower from his lapel. He lays
it on the table in front of her and then raises his head,
his eye catching a pair of old red leather slippers on the
floor by the door.

He says: Is Arthur coming?

She calls: Arthur? Arthur.

She revs up her legs for a bit, gets up, and begins to walk towards the side door.

He picks up her handbag and slides it onto the crooked right hand she holds out at her back.

When she arrives at the door she attempts to bend down and pick up Arthur's slippers.

The task is beyond her, so she exits.

He waits until she has gone.

He says: Though we have no children, we have many friends and a wonderful garden.

Arthur calls: *(From off.)* Norman?

Norman thinks Arthur is at the door and so he calls out to him.

He says: Arthur? Arthur? Arrrrr-thur?

He exits.

Arthur enters timidly through a different door. He is in full evening dress but has bare feet.

The big toe on his left foot stands eternally erect as if making a final and quite desperate bid for life.

He looks around for a bit and then heads towards the door through which Norman has exited.

Arthur calls: Norman?

Before he leaves, he flexes his ankle and briefly
examines his foot.

Arthur calls again: Norman?

Norman calls from off: Arthur?

Arthur exits towards the sound. Or so he thinks.

Norman enters.

He calls: Arthur? Arthur?

He works his way down towards the audience
and confides in them: Arthur is our dearest friend.
Actually... Actually, Arthur and Vee were...

A clock chimes.

He continues: Arthur and Vee... Arthur and Vee were engaged but he was shot in the war and suffered terrible amnesia.

Violet enters and he stops suddenly, not wishing to be overheard.

He puts a finger to his lips and looks at her as if expecting her to speak.

She notices his right hand is raised and thinks he's waving at her, although he's really cupping the hand to his ear as a signal that she should speak.

She waves back. Then she remembers she has something to say.

She says: We should thank Katy.

He says: Who?

She says: Katy

He announces: We would like to thank the caterers.

He searches for his phone using both hands, though they are evidently on separate missions.

He locates his glasses in the left outside breast pocket, puts the glasses on his face, gets a wad of cash from his outside left breast pocket, takes the glasses off his head to see the cash, stuffs the cash into his right bottom jacket pocket, goes inside the left breast pocket, feels something from inside, goes to the outside and locates his glasses case.

It's empty. He looks at the audience.

(III)

Norman puts his glasses case back into the pocket, raises his right hand to his head, reaches with his left hand to the pills case in his trousers, finds the glasses on his head and the pill case in his pocket.

He puts the pills down on table, tries to put his glasses away into a non-existent pocket, reveals a wad of cash, puts the cash away into the inside left breast pocket, the glasses away into the breast pocket, and then picks up the pills.

He shuffles to the table to take them with the water that is there.

He takes his Monday pills.

He picks up the glass of water in his left hand and drinks a little.

He says: What day is it?

She says: Wednesday

He turns the pillbox around so that the M of Monday is the W of Wednesday, and then turns it back again.

She oscillates imperceptibly behind him.

He takes his Tuesday and Wednesday pills.

He picks up the glass of water in his left hand and is just about to drink a little more when she says:

No, Friday.

He looks at his watch, turning his left wrist to do so and spilling the remaining water from the glass down his front.

He looks at the wet patch.

He puts the glass down.

He takes pills for Thursday and Friday (and maybe Saturday and Sunday as well), tips the whole lot into his mouth, day by day, chokes on them and coughs them up onto the floor.

(IV)

A dog comes on, eats the pills, sniffs around and then trots off. Her name is Onion and she has a spring in her step.

(V)

He says: Do you want a cup of coffee?

She laughs

He says: What?

She appears to say: Do you want to take your trousers off?

They laugh together, and then he goes off to get the coffee, feeling happy with himself. He takes the pillbox and glass with him.

She looks at her hands as if she is not certain they are her own.

He comes on with a full coffee cup on a saucer in his right hand, and a large napkin over his left arm.

(VI)

Some music comes on, like silent movie music, very fast, and their bodies instantly respond to it, like figures in a flickering old film.

He approaches her, balancing the cup and saucer.

She sits, alternately scratching her face and her groin.

Occasionally she turns to look at him.

He puts the coffee down on the table, flips the napkin out like a tablecloth and just as he does this the music stops.

He quickly places the coffee cup on the tablecloth at the far end of the table, opposite his wife, knowing that he has missed his cue.

She pulls the tablecloth towards her, moving the cup closer to her until the cloth dangles over the edge of the table.

If perchance he has a dangling thread of snot, he allows it to linger there until he gets his hanky out to catch it.

(VII)

He goes in for a kiss.

She leans back.

He reaches forward, leaning on the side of the table, his jacket hanging forward.

They pout at each other.

Their lips are almost on the point of touching when she averts her gaze to his crotch and undone fly, and the section of the shirt that's peeking out from it.

He observes her gaze and follows it, looking down.

She leans forward into him to sort the matter out.

His jacket obscures her face.

He looks out to the left wall that's facing him.

They stay in this position for a while.

His jacket falls back and his hand goes from resting on the fingers to his palm flat on the table.

He goes behind her.

She puts her left hand on the table.

He helps her stand up.

He puts her right hand on the table.

He goes behind her.

She puts her left hand on the table.

The lights go out.

(VIII)

When the lights come on there is a blob-like lilac-coloured thing. Gradually, vertebra by vertebra, and with none of its usual distortion or disfigurement, Violet's back emerges from the blob, the musculature moving subtly from side to side beneath the skin.

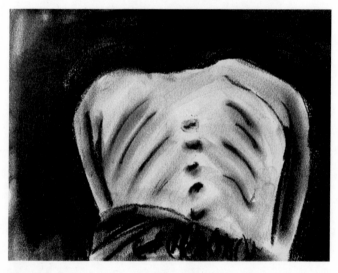

She slowly curls her spine back into it and floats off sideways to the door as a draping train unfurls blancmange-like at her rear, and Norman stares intently to the front.

(IX)

He speaks, filled with emotion suitable for the occasion:

We are gathered here today in memory of my wife, full
of anger and lust. Feeling hatred for anyone who does
not share our particular echo chamber of race, culture,
religion and hair colour, favourite poet. If we were truly
fearless, and I don't just mean on social media... Which
reminds me. There were some messages sent in.

He produces an iron crank, inserts it into the left-hand side of the table and begins to rotate it.

Once the table is opened to its fullest extent he takes out a large wad of paper from inside.

He closes the table up again. He looks for his glasses, finds his phone in the inside left pocket, transfers it to the inside right, finds money in the outside left top pocket, transfers it to the outside lower pocket, goes back to the inside left and finds his glasses.

He takes them out of the case, places the case on the table and puts on the glasses. He shuts the case and tries to put it in a nonexistent shirt breast pocket. Eventually he finds the inside left jacket pocket and puts the case in there.

He reads from the printout, though he often blurs and mumbles the messages (the ones in italics are picked out with clarity):

Thinking of you and your family at this terrible time… sending love…if there's anything you need please let me know…sending much love right now… *I'm so sad for you. What a blessing in this life to have been such a wonderful pair.*

My thoughts and prayers are with you hon. X

Aww Norman… *I'm not sure that she would welcome all the attention she is getting, but I know she would be amazed and embarrassed in equal measure by the outpourings of grief and sadness at her passing. I'm bewildered and confused by the sudden loss of someone so alive and present in the world – helpless in the knowledge that it is unfixable and without an answer…*

Sorry to see this sad news…*despite not knowing Vee…
or you…your news brought a tear to my eye… Oh wow…*
sending love to you now…you must be so proud…
much love to you, hope you find comfort in the
memories of family and close friends…my thoughts
are with you as you grieve…may beautiful memories…
so sorry to hear of Vee's parting big hug…thank
you for your post. Losing someone close is such an
incomprehensible and overwhelming experience. She
looks such a gorgeous and warm woman. How lovely
that you got to sing to her one last time. Sending you
massive love and hugs. I hope that you have a bit of
time out from everything. Thinking of you xxxx.

*It's funny, today is the anniversary of my wife's death, she
had a wonderful personality and stunning good looks – a
truly lovely lady whose father tragically hung himself…
(after two unsuccessful attempts with prescription drugs), her
brother abused her throughout her upbringing and after the
hysterectomy her cancer came as a blessing…*

Jesus Christ!

*If he was your saviour I'm sure would be thinking and
spending time with you now…and her in whatever form of
heaven you wish to cook up in your imagination.*

*We had so many laughs and good times and I never forget the
time when ner ner ner ner hugs and kisses*

A few more pages.

He flicks through the pages, probing deeper for
meaningful content and comes across a utility bill.

He says: N power.

As he examines the bill he holds up a handwritten page towards the audience which says something he wouldn't want made public.

Apparently referring to the N power bill, he says: Subliminal messaging.

He reads on.

I'm so sorry for this pain... I can't say she was more than an acquaintance to me, but I know that quite a few of you are mourning and hurting. Love to you if you are – and if you're not. Hold your loved ones close and make sure they know how dear they are.

Sending love to you. She must be so proud of the incredible person you are. Much love to you, and hoping you find comfort in memories, family and close friends From chicken and jam sandwiches to Norman – ringing from the other room.

So sorry to read this Norman. Maybe now is the time for us to get together. I always fancied you and I want to wrap my legs around you and smash my vagina into yours

My thoughts are with you as you grieve. May her beautiful memories keep you strong So sorry to hear of Vee's passing. Big hugs. You are a good boy! I was just thinking that you had been quiet on FB in the past few months, and wondered about Vee. I pictured you by her side. You lived a wonderful life and that's an amazing thing all by itself... X

I have such fond memories of Vee. Always gave the best cuddles and was so generous and welcoming. X Very beautiful words you have written there. Vee sounds great Big squeezey hugs & love coming your way. Xxxxxxx

So young, I remember her from when I would hang out at your house many moons ago. Much love I know this pain well. My heart wells up for yours. Xx

Ah dude that sucks

I have no words. Just love

I'll be watching over you every day. Making sure you hit your targets of blasting those abs. I am a big fan of hashtag smart bands. You can set them up anywhere and buy them from the link in my bio hashtag humpday.

Sending you loving caring healing energy.

She looks so IN that photo of you and her. Love to you all. Xx

Take care dear soul

Thoughts from afar to you xxx

Rather desperately longing to have a chat with this one x

Try it. Ask questions and listen for the answer.

I didn't live with my wife, only really got to know her cleaning up the house she died in, but I found that she'd put her two bobs into many situations, telling me stuff I didn't know, and being there for me. It was very interesting.

What a fucking fantastic woman. I miss him.

I also have no doubt that she was grateful for everything you did for her near the end, and that she loved your singing to her. Sending you all my love

I have regular chats with my gone loved peeps… Look for little signs, she's listening…xx

I just looked up the name Norman and it means a man with a tiny impotent prick

This is picture of you with a fish – didn't think it was possible for a man to be uglier than something he's caught

You've been a bit hasty and immoral, don't we think?

Massive bell-end in all fairness

You look like an Earthworm who's whacked a Hoodie on

Touché

Hah you legend!

Coming from the guy with 46 followers

Which appears to be 3 more than you. #ouch

The thing is I'm not abusing folk for likes ya bell end

You just have

0 replies 0 retweets 0 likes

End of conversation

Norman boy u the man

Haha owned total whalloper

There's always one little scrotum

Totally sums up some of my ex boyfriends

Touched a nerve there then. #banter.

Re-tweet this you filthy old slut.

Sorry to hear that Norman, all the best mate,

Hope you have some space with family to remember
and relive all the fun times. What a brave lady your
dear wife was!

I bet your pussy is disgusting.

*Arrest me! Sending hugs. I hope the knowledge that she's no
longer suffering sustains you through the next few days as you
celebrate her life* and share memories with all your family.

What a heart-wrenching tribute to a wonderful woman.
Hugs x

Oh my gosh sweetheart. I am so sorry. I have no doubt that
Vee was an amazing woman and her presence will be
missed in the world.

Big love and hugs to you. And Arthur.

(X)

Arthur enters. He is crying.

Norman says: Did you want to say something,
Arthur…?

Arthur approaches, sobbing inconsolably.

He collapses to his knees, taking an age over it, the air
rushing through the gaps between his fingers.

It's as if he's being sucked into the floor.

The lights go out.

(XI)

Norman is seated at the table eating his lunch – a plastic pot of seaweed salad – with a pair of chopsticks. The lid is to one side. There is a napkin and a dessert pot on a plate next to him.

Arthur is seated, crying.

Norman picks up one of the last strands of seaweed from his plastic tub and raises it towards his mouth.

He pauses with the chopsticks and seaweed poised as he watches Arthur weep.

A game of sorts ensues. Norman can only eat when Arthur isn't looking at him.

Norman puts the seaweed in his mouth.

Arthur cries even more.

Norman sucks his teeth, trying to dislodge some seaweed from a gap.

Arthur cries.

Norman finishes his salad, picking up individual strands of seaweed so that the pot is picked clean. He tries to replace the lid on the plastic pot, but has difficulty doing so. The lid seems to be slightly too small, but in his fumbling it flips over and he discovers it is an inlaid lid and it fits snugly the other way round. He puts it away under the table.

Arthur cries, extending his hands imploringly towards Norman.

He offers the napkin to Arthur.

Arthur takes the napkin. He dries his eyes then blows his nose.

He cries again.

Norman, meanwhile, peels off the plastic cover of the crème caramel and licks it clean, dabbing it with his tongue like a lizard.

He folds up the licked top and puts it on the table beside the chopsticks.

He tips out the pudding onto a plate so that it stands upright.

He realises he hasn't got a spoon and looks for one, first in his pockets and then in the drawers of the table.

He stands up. Arthur rises with him and extends an imploring hand.

Norman goes off to get a spoon, taking the chopsticks with him.

Arthur sits again, twisting his body to look at him.

Norman returns, minus the chopsticks but with a silver spoon.

The clock strikes one. Norman turns to look.

Arthur bobs down and rapidly sucks up the pudding in one gob-full.

Norman comes back to the table with a spoon in his right hand.

He sees the pudding has gone.

He picks up the empty plate in his left hand.

He drops the spoon on the plate.

He holds up Arthur's chin.

He slaps Arthur on the cheek.

He points at Arthur's face, moves away and turns his back.

Arthur, who's in profile, parts his lips.

There's a faint rumbling sound that seems to have its origin in his bowel. It travels up his alimentary canal, bypasses his oesophagus and emanates from his mouth, a painfully protracted croak.

When Norman hears it he joins in, exploding with the wailings of a recently bereaved seal.

The history they share has until this point been far too painful to discuss, but now, in these deep reverberations, they can discuss it. It's the tale of a woman loved by both, of a man going off to war and of a letter that will somehow, Arthur feels, explain it all.

Gradually the sounds decrease in volume and then stop.

Arthur moves back in his chair, the legs scraping on the wooden floor.

He stands and starts going through his pockets.

Norman moves towards him.

Arthur's hands travel from his own pockets to
Norman's, Norman's to his, and their delving turns into
a deeply felt embrace.

Then Arthur goes on tiptoe and his arms encircle
Norman's back and the fingers touch and the blood
begins to drain from him beginning with his toe and
Norman senses this and takes the weight and drags the
body of his friend towards the back and props him up
against the wall and as soon as Norman moves away
distracted by his mobile phone the limbs of Arthur
stir and an emaciated suited thing begins to twist and
turn across the wall and make its faltering contorted
way towards the door with arms raised high and legs
dissected like a damaged spider of the family Salticidae.

(*Arthonus*)

(XII)

We hear the dial tone. A series of beeps. Ring ring.

Thank you for calling N Power.

Calls will be recorded for training and monitoring purposes.

Please tell the representative if you don't want it to be monitored.

MUZAK

Norman undresses and sings along with the muzak. It is a 'Going home'/'In the Bleak Midwinter' medley.

Going home, going home, I am going home,
Quite like, some still day, I am going home.

Snow had fallen snow on snow, snow on snow.

In the bleak midwinter long ago.

Ring ring.

Norman thinks he's getting through, but he isn't.

Thank you. We are currently experiencing a high volume of calls. Please hold while we connect you to the next available operator.

MUZAK

He gets a shotgun and dog food and eats some dog food.

We apologise for the delay. Your call is important to us and we will connect you to the next available operator in approximately… three minutes.

MUZAK

Norman gets out a shotgun.

We apologise for the delay. We are currently experiencing a very high volume of calls. If you would like to receive a call back at a time convenient to you, please press 1. Or to speak to the next available operator, please continue to hold.

MUZAK

Norman cleans and loads the shotgun.

The clock chimes and Norman aims at it.

But just before it chimes, ring ring.

Norman shoulders the gun and accidentally fires it, knocking out a lighting fixture.

TELEPHONIST: Hello and welcome to N Power, you're speaking with Andrew. Can I start with your account number please? Hello? Hello?

NORMAN: Hello?

TELEPHONIST: Hello and welcome to N Power. You're speaking with Andrew. Can I have your account number please?

NORMAN: I want to close the account.

TELEPHONIST: This is your account, yes?

NORMAN: It is my wife's account. I'm calling you because she has died.

Silence.

TELEPHONIST: I'm very sorry to hear that, sir. Do you have her account number? Access to her emails?

NORMAN: I'm worried about cyber hacking.

TELEPHONIST: Cybo… Cyber hacking? OK, well in that case can you give me her name and her birth date please?

NORMAN: Her name?

TELEPHONIST: Yes, thank you, her name.

NORMAN: Her name was Violet

The lights go out.